The Occupant

Pitt Poetry Series

Terrance Hayes
Nancy Krygowski
Jeffrey McDaniel

Editors

The Occupant

Jennifer Maier

Published by the University of Pittsburgh Press, Pittsburgh, Pa., 15260
Manufactured in the United States of America
Printed on acid-free paper
10 9 8 7 6 5 4 3 2 1

ISBN 13: 978-0-8229-6739-2
ISBN 10: 0-8229-6739-1

Cover art: Ksenya Istomina, *The Quiet Life*, 2024. Collection of Galerie Bonnard.

Cover design: Alex Wolfe

for James

There is another world, but it is in this one.

—Paul Éluard

Contents

The Occupant

The Occupant Imagines the House as a Great Fish

It has already swallowed a century, each year a silver iridescent scale. For eight, she has lived in its belly, slightly beyond her means. How well she knows its creaks and currents of air, its slow, digestive rhythms. How many mornings she has stood behind the large, glassy eyes that stare impassively down on the park, observing the junkies and dog walkers awash in airy sunlight; and how many evenings felt herself sinking incrementally into the still and liquid night.

Sometimes she imagines the former occupants: the long dead whose bones are coral, or the others—dense spirits skimming the surface in narrow boats. She'd like to ask them a few things. *Why did you wallpaper the ceiling? Do you grieve for your body?* But their words, dissolved in air, can find no purchase here, and she is not yet proficient in the dialects of silence.

Still, there is no ill will. They come, untenable shadows, and go, stirring the boughs of tall firs. Today too the sun appears, birds call across the surface of the morning. *Song of dissolution, song of light.* She turns from the window as the thought rises—*the house is a fish, and I*—then glides into shadow, softly as the back door opening, closing.

Conch

She found me, a lacquered mouth
pressed to the lace hem of the sea,
turning fitfully in her dark arms
like a man going off to war.

Having no man of her own
she brought me home, held me
cool and hard to her ear. The things
I whispered cannot be told!

Now she is big with them.
I sit on her desk, trumpeting
my silence, pretending to be
a souvenir from Belize.

And she, cloud-fast, frequent
flyer, how could she know, ere
or since, she would sit tethered
to the kitchen table

scribe to the garrulous objects
of her household: these bodies,
heft and hum of the living world
that spins us here and gone—

the sunlight catching us
in its gold glance,
the shadow of night
letting us go.

Lingerie

Tidally
morning and evening, we slide
      into light—

sheer tentacles of stockings
      black cuttlefish of negligee

her fingers seining our salt sleep,
      these bras, scalloped in rows

the scuttling, four-clawed garter belt.
      Soft mollusk, chitin-less

what would she be without this
      borrowed armor

these fabricated fins of silk and lace,
      her tender lures

and stunning darts! And how many
      swimmers, their strokes

strong and sure, have we pulled
      down, held breathless

under the waves and carried in—
        alive and

gasping on the delicate strand
        of this world?

Matchbook

We are not the world,
we are the content of the world:
hazard and illumination—
          desire, consummation, ash.

And what you fear you must
apportion. We stand at attention,
twenty redheaded soldiers, a small company
awaiting your command:
one for the candle on your birthday cake
one to ignite a forest
one to spark Revolution
two for the chafing dish, the candelabra,
one to burn your bridges and another
for the shared cigarette after.

By all means, close cover
before striking. Hold us closely
in your two cupped hands.
Wherever we march cinders
into history. You'll know us
by our sulfurous traces—

smoke of your own days rising
behind you: last night
at the restaurant; the bright ships
of Carthage, burning.

The Occupant Considers Poisoning the Ants

For days she has watched them, one, a few, now a living pavement of black stones, crossing the white-tiled continent of the bathroom floor. They are smelling the way home to their nation in the masonry, to their bulbous queen, the molecular limit of being. To her they bring news of another world: food and crushing danger. The woman has been reading about the ants, how they forage far for what sustains them, go down into the earth again and again to bring up their dead. She unseals the box, studies the instructions in English and Spanish. *Ant grammar,* she reflects, *has no first person singular.* She applies the lethal drop to the paper with the red bullseye and sits down on the edge of the tub. Soon, one will smell the delectable poison, mark its place, and carry it back to the nest, her joy a fresh fuse of atoms burning behind her, the news smeared urgently on her sisters' bodies. Sooner still, the woman will retrieve the target, return it to the box, and close the flap. In some countries, she knows, this passes for mercy.

Mirror

Two truths approach each other. One comes from within,
one comes from without . . .

—Tomas Tranströmer, "Preludes"

One of you has come a long way,
walking years through desolate forests
and parking lots of broken glass.
The other has just arrived,
still pink from the shower,
on her way to the movies.

In me they meet face to face,
two strangers on a bridge
each speaking half a sentence.
This is how you recognize yourself,
how you slip singly over the border
of every future, avoiding detection.

Toothbrush

Day after day she takes me in
like a dull husband,
without love or regret,
moving hastily in circles
over the vaulted roof,
the small, vacant chairs
of the teeth, soft rug
of the tongue.
Then she returns me
to the cabinet
and offers her clean mouth
to the world,
that big shot who paces
behind her in the mirror
checking his phone.

Hairbrush

I was manufactured without irony:
    rounded head, 60 tufts of nylon bristles,

white plastic handle. The pink stripe bothers me,
    being inessential, for who among you

can withstand an encounter with pure Being? You
    flee or are turned to stone. Such is the purpose

of art, to decorate the fact and make it bearable.
    The stripe is a distraction of this kind.

What's more, though I labor to make you beautiful,
    I'm hidden in a drawer with the drab

elastic bands. Each day I am removed to smooth
    the ponytail the fingers twist into a small

neat loaf, pin carefully at the nape of the neck,
    then artfully destroy, to suggest the head

cares little for appearances. Therefore, in truth
    I have concluded that beauty is a lie.

Beyond that, Friend, I can say little, being made
    to keep silent and move solely in one direction.

Light Bulb

One day, eons from now,
brushing crumbs of earth from
this milky globe, tweezing out
the nerve-like filament

who, or whatever succeeds you
may pause to reflect that
Once, you were not
your own light. Then,

who among your vanished
race would not return—
retrace the long, unlit
hall to hold one again

in his animal hand,
recalling how you placed
them: low at the side
of the bed

or high on the walls
of communal spaces,
pale artificial moons
to draw back the tide of night

as it came to you then,
just an ordinary darkness,
filling your quiet stairwells,
your rose-scented yards.

The Occupant Recalls a Hymn by Isaac Watts
During a Rainstorm

O God, our help in Ages past,
Our Hope for years to come,
Our shelter from the stormy blast,
And our eternal home.

. . . .

Time, like an ever-rolling stream,
bears all its sons away;
they fly, forgotten, as a dream
dies at the opening day.   (1715)

Something in the wind has torn them loose, these verses blown back whole,
like planks from an abandoned ship. And with them the melody—calm
swells of the prelude collapsing into thunderous chords—dire interlude
through which Mr. Nye would steer the organ like a mad captain at the
helm, wresting it back toward that steady tetrameter when *God, Our Help*
would appear like a green island and they'd rise, mouths open, for that last
big breath before the *O*.

Ages past was the catch, she knew then, peopled by the Righteous, who
understood *His Word commands our flesh to Dust* and were okay with that, who
did not worry that the arrangement seemed kind of dicey, what her father
called an inside job.

Time, like an ever-rolling stream sounded nice, except as the means by which
The busy tribes of flesh and blood—meaning not just Indians, but everyone—
would be *carried downward and lost* when God gave the word. It would come,
the hymn promised, without warning, on some ordinary day like this one:

A thousand Ages in His sight like any other evening—*Gone*—like this evening, passing unremarkably, minute by minute, as the woman stands at the window, watching the gutters fill and the water lift and channel the dead leaves around parked cars toward the grate at the end of the street.

He'd have composed it in winter, she thinks. Spring floods were hopeful. She'd seen a frozen river break up in springtime—the current swift as a dream recalled suddenly in broad daylight, the past rushing by in pieces, carrying the dead back to their quiet rooms in some far-off desert country.

Red Paper Lantern

Ask me about love and impermanence.

They found me in Chinatown,
a collapsed lung with two wire ribs.
We opened at the same time.

Today I hang by the back door
waiting for rain. Something
with wings has entered me,

importunate, batting my sides.
I reply with a small squeak,
the sutra of the hook and the nail.

She is not trapped, only nervous.
She has forsaken the honeyed cell,
the maiden's vow of work

and rectitude. She thinks my
gold foil is the sun. Her shining
compound eye will not admit

the blue hatch overhead,
circle of sky that delivered her,
wanting only this red room

its rum circumference forever.
This is how the living enter love,
blind and questing

and remain, treading the air,
how they cling tightly
to love's paper armature

and call it *falling*.

Porcelain Buddha

Steadily, like rain
the hours filling two cupped hands
already broken

Eyeglasses

You think we offer you the world as it is,
without distortion, but this is a lie.

The world's doing just fine, thank you,
the verticals and horizontals still meeting

plumb at the corners, in sunlight and
deep shade; on the friendly letters of your

own name and on unacquainted objects
heaped in scrapyards. We're sorry

to be the ones to tell you that the source
of the *correction* you require to see

things clearly is, as usual, your own defect:
the astigmatic haze you walk around in

not to mention the blind self-regard
that would bend light itself to fit

your intimate refractions. We were
about to say such vanity costs nothing

that clarity removes some hazards by
revealing others. Take the view, just now

out the window: the myriad, sharp-veined
leaves of the vine maple, waving like

a green insurgency, or the sky, newly blue
without occlusion, like the clear eye

of a friend who says only what she means,
who replies truthfully when you inquire

about the surgery to make us obsolete—
We, whose lies unpuzzle the world

you take for real, who've been seeing
through you your whole life.

The Occupant Contemplates Selling the Family Heirloom

Lately she's been wondering if it should start over with someone else:
ANTIQUE SIDEBOARD, OAK, WITH THREE DRAWERS, TWO CABINETS,
AND REMOVABLE MIRRORED BACKSPLASH—and whether the bad would
go with it, written in the grain, as trauma on the rings of a tree; trapped
behind glass, like ghosts in a jar. *Tiger oak*, they'd said, though the child
felt no terror in the dark striations, the surface dashed like little hairs, or
in the carved claw feet that couldn't scratch or run away. STURDY, WITH
ORIGINAL BRONZE HARDWARE—a low, solid wall you could crouch
behind, like a TV cop caught in the crossfire; wide, curved handles that
could support a kid's weight, could save a kid if she fell through the ice,
plunging down into black water so cold you wouldn't even feel it when you
drowned. LOVINGLY KEPT BY THE SAME FAMILY SINCE 1915—*kept*, like
a secret, those three strong consonants like the click of the lock she'd turn
quietly on the front door when he was out in the truck with a gun and a
bottle. OLD INK STAIN IN TOP LEFT DRAWER, stark outline of a lake she
can no longer name, at whose frozen edge they'd all lived a long time ago.

Cup and Saucer

Columbine, Haviland-Limoges, 1902

We know that to survive, lovely
and unbroken, would be *your* choice

but listen when we tell you: Some things
are worse than shattering. We speak

from the shade of the high cupboard—
cool, silent, like the death you fear.

And why? Aren't you, like us, composed
of bone and clay, fired to a near-translucency?

The tip of your finger held against the sun
proves this; the ground, your good, first

home, will not turn you away. Plant us
there, why don't you? We'll talk among

the Ladies who recall, better than you,
all we contained when once we were

a woman's choice, conferred by the gold
band. Then, pattern was all—it was herself

held poised and steady in a white-gloved
hand. Festoons of roses on cerulean ground

or wreaths of ivy, scenes of old Cathay,
the voluptuary ease of summer gardens

in whose round world the hour might be
comforted—not real, but as real might

have been, each false flower petalling forward
in slow time. That stopped with you.

And now we bloom alone at night behind
the cupboard door, shrouded in newsprint

neither soft nor fine and buried in a carton
from the liquor store.

The Occupant Assesses Her Current Condition, Consistent with Age and Use

The maker's mark has faded and is no longer legible. Since news of a friend's death last week, she has developed a hairline crack, running from a point behind her left ear all the way to the sole of her foot. Not long ago she was badly chipped when a lover dropped her for someone else. Yesterday she broke her small toe, hurrying to answer the phone in case it was him, sick with regret and pleading for a second chance—a minor defect that in no way affects her stability. Despite these losses, she thinks she looks fine when viewed from her good side. She is still usable, able to hold nearly as much as before.

Pleasure Object

That which you cannot name you euphemize,
hand out as door prizes at bachelorette parties.
And this is your whole problem.

If I were capable of shame, I'd blush, & not
—as one like you surmises—at "the nature
of my work," but your efforts to conceal it.

Set me on the mantel beside the little Buddha
& we'll see whose magic is more powerful, press
the appeal of Right Intention up against Desire.

Think opposites attract? *Ix-nay* on that.
Your choice is clear: the dusty one on his high
shelf or me, myself, the ergonomic genie

of a grand hotel, in whose long-lasting charge
the coiled thread of every silken pleasure unfurls
at your command. My lamp's your *head*

& there too, close at hand, is every woman
you can name—virgin, stripper, cloistered nun—
who waits there in her numbered room

for every man she ever wanted:
that stranger at the hardware store,
the groom.

Eight Things the Occupant Thinks About While Making a Cake and One That Does Not Occur to Her

1. Whether it's possible to step figuratively out of one's body, observe oneself with the detached neutrality of a stranger.

2. Probably not.

3. Whether some *other* person—e.g., a stranger from the future—seeing her framed here, in the serene light of the kitchen window, beside this orange digital scale, this scattering of currants on the counter, would feel the same prick of ineffable sadness she felt observing Vermeer's *Woman Holding a Balance* last week at the museum.

4. Yes. What kind observer would *not* be moved at the sight of the pensive baker—herself!— ringed by the quaint tools of her craft, and who, though centuries dead, is quickened in this moment of perception?

5. Even so, the objects that survived her—the rubber spatula, the yellow mixing bowl—now housed in the museum's 21st-century collection, speak only of their time, while those in Vermeer's painting seem undying: the instrument itself, held light and empty in the woman's hand, the coin-like weights and heavy ropes of pearls that spill from the box beside her, too large, certainly, for the balance to contain.

6. Of course, for the people of Delft, these things—along with the miniature *Last Judgment* that Vermeer hung on the wall behind her—would have testified to his subject's place, poised between this world and the next, where her life, like theirs, would be measured grain by grain; while the less eloquent tools in *Woman Making a Cake* may only recite the facts of mankind's deathless love of sweet confections.

7. On one side cake; on the other, the resurrection of the body.

8. That on the wall behind her is a mirror, which seems significant, though she cannot decide if it is a sad significance or a happy one, or whether the stranger, in the light of her own time, would see in it a plenitude or a void.

9. That while the woman has been weighing these things, the mirror has been painting the back of her head, the flour sifting softly into the yellow bowl, the five panes of the kitchen window, the green tops of trees, and, minute by minute, the singular colors of the day going down and the night rising to meet it.

Whisk

My business is amalgamation—
what do I know?
I stand with the Utensils,
a small steel cage
without a heart,
while the keeper of
the mad hand that moves me
lives single and apart—
an unbroken egg—
and is not sorry
or is glad.

Kitchen Knife

I chop, crush, peel, serrate; what God has joined,
together we unmake. Your helpmate and accom-
plice, I should know—what good's an onion
whole, except to throw? A knapped flint was
the first machine. Then, you supplied the
motive, I, the means. But now I'm under-
utilized. It seems that since our forays in
the Forum, you've lost your edge, &,
governed by decorum, now murder
only to dissect; you cut with words
& wound with "disrespect." It's
bad enough for me; for you it's
worse—parsing your days like
parsley, a garnish for the
hearse. If time's a line,
let's cleave it out of
joint. We might
do more—okay?
This is my
p-o-i-n-
t.

The Occupant Is Visited by the Dead Poet

This is not strictly true. She brought him home, right over the threshold in her blue and white striped bag. Something in the author photo on the back had moved her—the V of his white shirt, open at the neck like a lily; the cigarette held slack between long fingers, tipping to the ground. His face wore an expression she knew: bold, yet tender, the way a man looks just after one thing and before something else. When he died—young, suddenly—Bill Clinton was the president.

She read every poem, even the long, strange ones. Her favorite was about the possum and her other favorite about the two trees. When she finished it was dusk, and the leaves were full of plaintive sounds.

What do you think? he asks, and she tries to explain how reading the poems was like falling into a ravine, rolling down a canyon, and waking up in another body—one with claws and fur and a nose that could read the air.

That's good, he says, *write that down. What else?*

I think you shouldn't have smoked.

Move me to your bed, he says, *and I don't mean the nightstand.* She does this, slipping the book under the sheet, next to her.

Is this how it's going to be? she asks.

What else? he replies.

Days pass. Soon they are living together, but the woman is not happy. For one thing, the poet keeps leaving his beautiful words all over the place, on top of her own things. Also, she is insecure. How do you please a man with no body? She feels large, hulking around the house. He tells her they're lucky, there is no intimacy like theirs.

Sometimes they argue. She worries he's using her. One day she says, "Is this what you do now, pick up women in bookstores?"

What else? he replies.

And although she says nothing, in these words the woman perceives the wound—coiled, breathing—at the center of her love, this wound at the center. Since then, she has been making a place for it in the wilderness, where, in time, they may meet again without impediments, and all will be possible, as in dreams. But not today. It is still too early for that.

Moth Orchid

Phalaenopsis Amabilis

Because your roots are purely metaphorical,
your feet planted crudely on packed soil,
you incline toward airy associations.

Why else compare us to that drab animal
ravaging your closets, a fool for any
naked bulb? Look at it now,

its abdomen pressed to the window,
romancing the cold moon! At least those
Greeks your botanists are so enamored of

devised a way to tell false light from true.
God in a shower of gold? He comes to *you*.
Mornings, in our case, when our pallid need

has stirred him out of sleep, and he climbs
hot and high through the kitchen window,
filling us lip and tendril, budding us stalk

by stalk. We understand it's different
with your kind—hurried and in darkness—
thirsting to be known as we are known.

Think of us as a crowd of white faces
who've seen this and more: watched
you lie down in his bright beam

that you might be entered like that
and rise, with his heat in your hair,
dimly conceiving.

Glass of Wine

Forget half full, half empty.
You people always ask the wrong questions.

Forget *veritas*. Also women and song.
Let us not raise a toast to time past
or to come, or the good bright dog
running between them, another hour

dropped slick in the palm of your hand.
Why else but to ease that panting animal
do you reach for this at the end of the day,
in some noisy bar, surrounded by friends

or alone at your desk by the window,
as tonight, the woman brings the glass
to her lips, thinking first of what must
be done tomorrow, and later

of the new neighbor, who returns late
from the office. It pleases her to see
his tall silhouette, tipped in the light
of the front porch, and the way

his gym bag hangs from his shoulder
like a hunter's quarry. Sip by sip
the hour shall find them, on a hill
outside Montepulciano

laughing at how they met, years before,
when her dog strayed into his yard
after a ball. And what does it matter
that he has a wife, and she,

only a fish circling its small glass
bowl? Silently, I open the gate, and
the animal roams where it will, bright
on the trail of impossible longings

till reason calls it home. Witness
the dog, the man, the rust-colored hills
into which he will soon fade, like the saint
recalled to tame the wolf

that has devoured another villager
and must be taught to live, chaste and
hungry, in the gnarled forest of
circumstance, where he belongs.

Black Molly

Genus Poecilia, a common aquarium fish

In the right light, I'm more of a deep violet.
      I swim in circles, careful to turn always at

the last minute, before the sea brittles
      into mystery, that sheer surface on which

the dull brown snail writes its name over and
      over, the prayer of the small-souled animal.

Outside, God in the dangerous air. See how she
      loves us, bringing day, then night

then day. Reliably, gold flakes fall from her
      hand, linger on the surface and drift

down—past the complacent snail, past the green
      frond swaying like a dropped

bow line, all the way to the deck of the little broken
      schooner, that must have thought

it could sail right through the clear, hard pane
      of the world to reach her.

After a Period of Sadness, the Occupant Wakes from a Happy Dream

She must have carried them with her: the long griefs folded end-to-end; the facts, stacked in unassailable layers; each small regret tucked discretely out of sight

because when she awoke, it was all there—the latched case sprung open now, its contents littering the ground, or caught and hanging from high places, as from the limbs of a tree

and something rushing away from her, the face like a familiar city glimpsed below clouds, its fine distinctions vaporous—going—

Or *staying*, rather, in the country of Before, where he'd moved some time ago and now was safe and well, as she was *here*,

waking in fractured sunlight, in the warm salt marsh of her own land. One of the lucky ones, with the smell of gasoline, and small fires burning all around.

Alarm Clock

Because you seek your image in all things,
     the part you call my *face* is round,

 though dark as the night sky. At its curved
     edge, numbers glow in the places

you've ordained for them. By these
     you chart your course, hourly, through

nothingness: twelve candles raised against its
     fathomless infinities, as men mapped

the stars so as not to drown there. My hands,
     too, are complicit in your fictions: the short

slow and the long fast one, and the fixed red arm
     that delivers the morning. Like the knife

they slice your life into morsels, to fix on the tines
     of your fork. How like you not to see

 that even I, untouched by time, can't keep it.
     Some days I want to drop my hands

in futility at the way you equate passing with
     dissolution: each tick a small erasure,

like the beat of your own heart: *one less,*
      one less. And have you ever stopped to think

not even you can *spend* a thing you can't possess?
      That while you're busy portioning infinity,

each second breaks like a salt wave at your feet
      and returns to the sea, which is only ever

the *now*—alive and infinite. This is what time tells *you:*
      the fact I whisper 60 times per minute

but that you will not hear. You and the others,
      roused to waking only by my screams.

Bed Pillow

White feathers, plucked and gathered.
Why should you wonder
at the sensation of falling, the dreams
of something lost, *taken?*

It's time you knew.
Nightly, I carry you, rising
and falling in soft waves,
each breath a wingstroke—

the hours of the morning
and the hours of the afternoon,
scattered hay wheels; broad fields
receding behind us.

Next, the chartless Interior
with its dry plains, its puzzled forests—
stopping now and then at some
half-remembered outpost

with its own ways, loud,
and peopled with animals,
or the dead who turn up like
boozy locals, not making sense.

How deftly you master their language
of gestures, their quick tongues
without past or future. And so
we might travel forever—

clear to the far shore—but always,
the urge for return that is your
affliction, an excess of love
for the world you call real.

One night soon I'll keep going.
Remember to turn back at
the fourth hour, then look for
the angled roof, the green door

coming into view, and the frail
husk of the body that wakes
daily its narrow bed, grateful
again for the life you *have*,

while the wonders we lived,
moments ago, drown splashless
in your first cup of coffee,
the first song on the radio.

The Occupant Is Knitting an Infinity Scarf

A closed loop with two sides and no discernible end, like a circular argument.

Good for the novice knitter, the yarn lady said, setting the soft skeins on the counter. Two gray shades, Granite and Feather.

The woman wonders if she has taken up knitting because she has no children, wishing to work some strand of her life into the lives of other women, back to the beginning. She imagines them standing in a circle around her, clad in sweaters coarse and fine and the colorful hats of the Ages. Their patience is endless, as shown by two anonymous hands in the video *Knit an Infinity Scarf!* which she replays over and over to review the technique.

Soon—in no time at all—she is knitting & purling, purling & knitting; the tips of her needles moving expertly, like the teeth of sheep browsing the lap of her own yard; and beyond, in the raveling distance, flocks cropping grass in Sabine hills, in the rock-strewn remnants of Troy and Carthage.

Any day now the woman will finish the infinity scarf, sealing the two ends into a riddle, which she'll twist and slip over her head. Then they'll step out together: she and two shorn lambs, Granite & Feather, and the woman will see her breath, white, seamless, in the sharp winter air and sense the weight of the past, linked to the present in an unbroken chain of events, and carry it with her, the way people do.

Spider

Let x be the distance from lamp to windowsill,
and y from sill to ceiling.

Let x be long patience and y, eternal hazard:
a green lacewing, an open door.

The rest is a story spun from memory—
its spiral threads and radial threads,

silk of the hammock that has rocked
so many. The lacewing approaches.

Where she lands will mark the Day,
the Hour. She is a summer afternoon,

and my venom the shadow of night
filling her body. Below, the woman

flits about the room, doing what she will.
Today she is knitting a scarf—

not as my namesake, in her Greek
perfection, but clumsily, from

instructions. I am the Watcher in the corner
she does not kill, thinking herself

advanced. What does she know of death's
soft steps, its solemn reciprocities? She

with one good hand and a single pair of eyes
that can see only what's in front of them.

Dust Bunny

My form is soft,

    mammalian,

        though I have swallowed

    the whole of you—

your past, weightless

        and particulate,

    and the future

that reaches out to stroke

        the delicate, pink shell

    of your ear,

slowly, day after

    day, so as not

        to frighten you.

Passing a Cemetery, the Occupant Briefly Considers Forms of Posthumous Existence in Which a Trace of the Individual is Preserved

Dust, first.

And the slow diminuendo of descendants, cached in the future like nested dolls. Diaries. Bundled letters in listing script.

Film stars, safe in their cinematic gestures: the moment between lighting a cigarette and the white plume of smoke that means trouble.

Recorded voices; text messages one cannot yet erase.

"Artistic products"—*viz.*, poems, plays, and the like—fine enough to endure, but not so great as to eclipse the author. Notable exceptions considered in turn.

Unhappy ghosts/restive spirits, etc., whose shade the living wander into and feel cold.

The dead depicted in paintings and photographs, who know now, but may not tell.

Infamy, for a while. And sainthood, though not one point on the filament between them.

These Sleepers, all changed. Dandelions flaring here and there on the broad lawn.

Their flight in air, their silvery ascension.

Sunflower

Truly I say you're no different
from the finch, the chickadee,
the eye picking always
for beauty and the mind,
beak and claw, for sustenance.
And flight is flight—
Why should I care who consumes me?
The sun called me out
of the dirt and I came forth
to blaze and testify.
And here, browning in a dry vase
on the counter, I tell you
it's true: death is only a change
of worlds, a second opening.
Take this stalk
broken for you, this heart
riven into images:
Dilated eye of summer
Eclipse on a stick
Corazon Sagrado,
deposed from a grove
of patient prophets,
each head bowed,
each crowned with thorns.

Bowl of Cherries

Wanting the whole truth
as you say, even you've got to admit
there's no room for sadness here:
Some things are just plain good.

We know that kind of messes you up,
that even now you're thinking,
Yes, but what *else* are they?

It's the blight of your kind—
the way you go straight to the brain,
that walnut whose fruit's

all on the inside, when it ought to be
the other way around. Then
there would be no surprises,

the goodness there for all to see,
and the little stone at the center
coming freely away, like those

you're tossing into the hedge,
mindlessly, as you puzzle out how
everything is like some other thing,

when, really, it's not.
Trust us: the truth ripens and falls
and its sweetness stains the ground.

You're holding it now, lightly
between two fingers.
Your tongue is red with it.

Memorandum

We have some reason for concern,
but not the hearts for it.
Things that don't die see clearly,
having nothing to fear from the end of use,
no reason to invent indemnities.

Much of the time she stares out
the window, or sits motionless under
 the ochre eye of the table lamp, beside
stacks of books written by others,
smarter and more industrious than she.

Among the appliances, her favorite
is the espresso machine, followed by
the new German vacuum cleaner.

Sometimes she spends whole mornings
re-arranging objects on the mantle
and whole afternoons putting them back.
In this she is perfectly happy.

We've often observed her in the kitchen,
making soups from wholesome ingredients,
or talking to friends on the phone,
pleased to know they will meet soon,
but not today.

She worries frequently that
she is too much alone and that this
doesn't worry her as it should.

Don't ask us how we know,
but she believes that, given the chance,
she could have made Chekhov
fall in love with her, nursed him
through his long and terrible illness,
and gone to live happily at his
country estate, where they'd smile
to think he had ever said,
If you fear loneliness, don't marry.

In the shower she sings hymns
that describe heaven as a pure
and shining river, believing her
preference for oil-slicked, brackish
shoals and abject places unfits her
for any religion.

She wonders if she will die
in the pale blue bedroom, and if so
whether her soul will slip softly from
her body like a sated lover, or in some
other way she likes to imagine,
or not at all.

The majority concedes it would be better
if she were less like herself and more
like the Others in paintings and
photographs—those who, at the end
of use, may now reside forever
safe in their cold country.

We therefore advise the timely cessation
of all breathing human passion, etc.,
though we are not optimistic.

The Occupant Revisits the Rooms of Her Life and Arrives at a Late Understanding

Sometimes she imagines it will happen this way / that it has happened already and she stands remembering / that it is happening now amid the songs and the silences of night and in the dawn of her imagining—her body a wisp of air in the long corridor, stirred in the wake of her passing.

Then, as before sleep, she will move through the rooms, shutting the lamps off one by one: cities, loves, animals, all the nights and days dissolving in air behind her

until she stands light and alone among solid things, indifferent witnesses that persist without memory, though they furnished its many rooms. Her hand moved them, as she herself was moved—*drawn,* by something apart from them. Cold clarity of a knife blade; glint of sun on the rim of a glass.

Some action seems required of her: some provision made for these durable goods, her possessions. She would return them with a note of thanks:

The French oak desk to the wild pigs of the Midi, who foraged in its absent shade

The feather home to the goose, and the conch to its salt terrain

The red rug to the yurt-- to the ewe-- to the wild grass of the Caucasus

Back to bone and silica the china; this silk to the mulberry leaf

Each forged thing to its atomic weight, its elemental body

But they will not go. Time is flowing forward again; sunlight gilding this still room in the house of the mind that deplores a vacancy as, then and now, the Occupant looks up from her writing to trace particles of dust drifting everywhere in air, alighting on every surface.

Acknowledgments

My thanks are due to the following publications, in which some of these poems first appeared:

> *Plume:* "The Occupant Imagines the House as a Great Fish" and "Eight Things the Occupant Thinks About While Making a Cake, and One That Does Not Occur to Her"; *Gettysburg Review:* "Moth Orchid," "Light Bulb," "Bowl of Cherries," and "Glass of Wine"; *Southern Humanities Review:* "Mirror"; *Christianity and Literature,* "Black Molly" and "Sunflower"; *Tiny Spoon,* "The Occupant Is Knitting an Infinity Scarf."

"The Occupant Imagines the House as a Great Fish" is also reprinted in *What the House Knows,* edited by Diane Lockward (Terrapin Books, 2025).

I am also grateful for grants and fellowships from Seattle Pacific University and The American Academy in Rome, where my stays as a visiting writer in 2023 and 2024 helped greatly in the completion of this book.

Finally, I'd like to thank the many friends, colleagues, and students who've offered advice and encouragement along the way, including Ed Ochester, Phillis Levin, Sharon Bryan, Scott Cairns, James Fritz, Nicole Miller, and Barbara Geary Truan.